The Three Jaguars Present:

From Spark to Finish: Running Your Kickstarter Campaign

M.C.A. Hogarth

The Three Jaguars Present:
From Spark to Finish:
Running Your Kickstarter Campaign

First edition, copyright 2012 by M.C.A. Hogarth

All rights reserved. No part of this publication may be reproduced, stored in a retrieval system, or transmitted, in any form or by any means, electronic, mechanical, photocopying, or otherwise, without the prior written permission of the author.

M. Hogarth
PMB 109
13176 North Dale Mabry Blvd
Tampa, FL 33618

ISBN-13: 978-1479379705
ISBN-10: 1479379700

Cover and interior art by M.C.A. Hogarth

Designed and typeset by Catspaw DTP Services
http://www.catspawdtp.com/

Table of Contents

Introduction 1
1. First Things First: Is My Project Right for Kickstarter? 2
2. Am *I* Right for Kickstarter? 5
3. Design. 8
4. Running Your Campaign. 23
5. Fulfillment 30
6. All Done? Do it Again 34
7. From Spark to Finish Checklist 35
About the Author. 37

Introduction

My first Kickstarter project, to launch a military science fiction novel, overfunded 234% in thirty days; I asked for $1500 and got $3519.

My second project, to launch an urban fantasy novel, overfunded 111% in thirty days; I asked for $1500 and made $1665.

My third project, an offer to draw little doodles for people in return for enough money to buy some new markers, overfunded 589% in ten days; I asked for $300 and made $1768.

My fourth project, to launch a fantasy of manners novel, overfunded 414% in thirty days; I asked for $1500 and made $6221.

⇒ ◆ ⇐

My name is M.C.A. Hogarth. I'm an indie writer and illustrator, and I am not a superstar. In fact, as such things go, I'm a pretty average fish in a pond a lot of people aren't aware of . . . ! But I started using Kickstarter in 2012, and it has revolutionized my revenue model, and by revolutionize I mean it's over doubled my income. Kickstarter has allowed me a luxury rarely afforded freelancers and independent artists: capital to fund their projects in advance, and maybe even put some food on the table while they're working. It's been so useful for me that, as you can see, I've done it four times already, and I've already got the next two or three projects lined up, some following formulas that have worked before, and some experiments so I can find some things that work better in the future.

I've learned a great deal in my year on Kickstarter. I can't tell you how to use it to become the next J.K. Rowling or Felicia Day. But the methods I've put down in this book have worked for me, and I'm hoping they work for you . . . because the world needs more people following through on their dreams and adding fantastic, beautiful, thought-provoking, or just plain awesome things to the world. I back five to six Kickstarter projects for every one one I launch and I'm always finding exciting new things to spend my coffee money on.

I'm hoping the next one I back . . . will be yours! So let's get to work!

First Things First:
Is My Project Right for Kickstarter?

I HAVE SEEN THE FOLLOWING things on Kickstarter:

1. A project to fund the creation of a secret sauce for hamburgers.
2. A project that existed to let people pre-register for a new gaming convention.
3. Multiple projects asking for people to fund travel so that someone can go someplace beautiful and take photos/make a documentary/write stories in a log cabin somewhere.
4. A project soliciting money so that a web comic artist could take the paid ads off the site for a year.
5. Projects to build community spaces to play in (parks), cook in (community kitchens) or make art in (photography studios/open live modeling sessions/dance spaces/etc).

And this is just the tip of the iceberg. The breadth of projects being funded through Kickstarter is unbelievable, and it's a rare day on the site where I don't run across someone doing something new, unusual or interesting.

From my observation, then, this is the formula that makes an appropriate Kickstarter project:

You have an interesting **urge** *that results in* **creative**

products *that can be awarded to people, that you can tell a fun and compelling* **story** *about, and that fits in a Kickstarter* **category.**

That's it.

Your urge is to travel to Italy to sample wine? And you're good at photographing things? Then you have a photography project. Your story is how much you love wine and how excited you are about Italy. Your products could be anything from a thumb drive of stock photography captured on your trip to signed postcards mailed from wherever you were with a personal hand-written story addressed to your backer.

Your urge is to make onesies for babies for reading geeks? You have a fashion project. Your story is that you love kids and you love books and you just know there are other parents who want to dress up their kids in fashion that reminds them (when they are changing them for the umpteenth time) that when they're done there's always a book to relax with. Your products are the designs—maybe you just want to sell the designs and people can put them on their own products—or the onesies themselves.

Your urge is to draw! But you have no idea what. You have an art project. Your story is that you love to draw and you want to connect with your audience. Your product is little bits of art, from very tiny to very large, depending on what level people back at.

Your urge is to do world-building. You have a publishing project. Your story is that you're fabulous at making up realistic, immersive settings for people to play in. Your product could be anything from PDFs of information people can use in roleplaying games to licenses to use your setting in their fiction to weekly emailed "newspapers" from your universe, telling people what's going on that week.

⇒ ◆ ⇐

Your only limit here is your imagination. You want to go to a comic convention but don't have the money to travel? What could you give people in return for funding your trip there? Why not offer to take photos for them of their favorite creator/cosplay costume? You could offer to sit on panels they'd like to attend and live-tweet the results for them. If you can come up with a creative way to reward people for something you want to do, then you're good to go . . . as long as Kickstarter approves it! But then, they have approved some strange and interesting things, so don't make the decision for them. Be gutsy, pitch it to them and let them make the call.

Your best starting point—and I will say this more than once—is to go to the Kickstarter site, choose the creative category that best matches yours (for me, those are Art and Publishing; for you they may be Design, Photography, Food, Film & Video, etc. . . .), and then browse. See what other people are trying to do. See what they're offering as prizes. *Take notes.*

As they used to sing in Epcot's Horizons pavilion: If you can dream it, then you can do it. So why not try?

Chapter One Questions

1. What would I really love to do? What creative project have I been crazy to do?

2. What kinds of things would I make as a result of that creative project? A book? A film? Designs? A machine? A recipe? A collection of recipes?

3. Why should other people be excited about what I want to do? What about it makes it unique? What about me makes me interesting and worth supporting? Why should they really want the things I'll be making?

4. What Kickstarter categories are there? Where does my project fit?

Am I Right for Kickstarter?

So you've got a project in mind; you think the story is compelling and the rewards intriguing. Your next question is . . . are *you* right for Kickstarter?

Here's the hardest lesson I had to internalize about Kickstarter: unless you're a superstar (or very lucky), Kickstarter is not your lottery ticket. Just posting a project's not going to make a herd of strangers rush out of nowhere to make your dreams come true. So here's the number one thing I've observed to be true of myself and others:

Kickstarter projects energize your current fanbase. You can count on no more than 10% participation from Kickstarter's browsers, and 5% is more likely. If you can't get much money out of your existing base, you shouldn't pin your hopes on your Kickstarter project doing so.

So what does that mean? Should you not try at all? Of course not! But recognize that if you're someone with few fans and no name, you should maybe table your $20,000 "fund my writer's retreat so I can write at my leisure for a year" project and try something a little more modest instead. If you have ten fans and run a successful Kickstarter campaign, then according to the numbers, you're going to reach one new person.

Do that again.

And again.

Ten percent isn't much. But for most people, overnight

success takes a decade to cultivate. You can get started now!

The key, then, is to be realistic about the amount of money you can expect. If over the past month you've earned $10 from people paying you for your creative work, try to come up with a project with a goal in the hundreds of dollars, rather than the thousands. Keep in mind that success intrigues people; if you ask for $100 and end up with $200, you will attract the interest of people who wonder what everyone's so interested in. If you ask for $100 and end up with $1000, I guarantee that strangers browsing the site will want to know what's going on. It pays to think small, especially at first. Big projects can fire people's imaginations, but unless you're already a known, it really is like buying a lottery ticket.

So think small and nimble . . . and repeatable. Your goal is to be able to launch another project quickly, to keep your name fresh. Take that "fund my writer's retreat for a year" project. Instead of planning it as a single project, take it apart: "fund my writer's retreat for a week." Suddenly you only need $385, and that's a lot more do-able, isn't it?

The other important thing about the Kickstarters-energizing-your-base observation is the word "energize."

You know where that energy comes from?

You.

If you're not excited about this project, if you're not committed, if you're not bursting at the seams with enthusiasm that you *must* share with people about how awesome this is going to be and how you can't wait to do this with other people's help, and how we're all in it together and it is going to be amazing . . . if you're not that super-excited about it . . . shelf it and find something you are excited about. Because without your passion, your dedication and your enthusiasm, your project will launch like a lead balloon. Running a Kickstarter campaign takes a lot of time and energy, and because you'll be counting on your fans and backers to help you spread the word, you need to be convincing about why they should: why they should like the project, why they should help you and not a dozen other people like you. You need to set them on fire! And make them feel like part of your team. Because they are, and they will be.

If you don't have the drive, they will conclude that you're not going to deliver on your promises. Worse, they'll feel like they're taking their hard-earned money, which they are excited about sharing, and giving it to someone who doesn't care. It's a terrible rejection. Honor their gifts. If you feel you can't because you're just not too into what you're offering . . . then go back to the drawing board until you find something worth your living energy, and theirs.

Chapter Two Questions

1. Do I have fans yet? Supporters? How many people know about my creative aspirations and projects?

2. Do I make any money yet on my creative projects? About how much a month? A year? A project?

3. Do I have a strong social media presence, or know people who do? Am I willing to invest the energy in having one?

4. Am I really excited about this project? Am I committed to it? Can I throw myself into advertising it for ten to sixty days?

Design

So you've got a project in mind, you're excited, you're ready to start! Your first step is designing your campaign. Campaign design goes beyond filling in all the blanks on the Kickstarter site and hitting "launch." Before all that, you need your trusty pen and paper (or whatever you use for ideas). It's time to sit down and *plan*!

Research

As I mentioned in a previous section, your first task is to do research. Pull up the Kickstarter website and explore the categories that your work might fit into. Investigate the currently funding projects. Check out the Most Popular/ Most Funded projects. Have a look at Recently Successful and Staff Pick projects. What are their creators doing? Are there endeavors similar to yours? What seems to be working for their creators? How did they pitch their idea to potential backers? What are they offering as prizes? Try calculating what it would cost you to offer similar rewards. Can you do it? Look around at projects that interest you. What caught your eye? Did any of the prizes strike you as irresistible or creative or compelling? Jot those down.

So now you have a sense for what other people are doing, and what you could do yourself. But not all creative professionals are good with numbers—witness one project where someone offered to send a handmade bracelet to every backer who pledged $5. That person lost a lot of money fulfilling her promises to her backers . . . !

So on to step two.

Calculating the Price of Your Project

Now it's time to figure out how much you need. Once you know that, you'll know how much you should ask for—and no, they're not the same thing! Say your goal is to take a trip to Alaska to paint wild birds for your portfolio. Break out the spreadsheet (or notepad) and start itemizing everything you'll need for the trip. And I do mean everything. For your birding expedition, for instance:

1. Airfare, round-trip, with associated fees for luggage/tax/etc.
2. Lodging.
3. Food budget.
4. Event money—you're going to paint birds, but how are you going to see them? Have you booked a tour somewhere? Are you visiting a zoo? Going to a national park? Does the park have an entrance fee? Are you going to camp there? Do you have camping supplies? How much do those cost?
5. Miscellaneous: do you even have clothing for cold weather/marshes? Wrack your brain by imagining yourself going on this trip. What are you doing? What might you have forgotten?
6. Materials: how much paper are you packing to paint

on? How about sketchbooks? How much are your pencils? How much is your paint? How much are you planning to use, and what's the per-item cost?

Say you add up all these things and come up with $3000. That's just for you to take the trip, paint, and come home, flushed with excitement.

Guess what: you can't ask for $3000, or you won't make it there.

Hidden Costs

First off, for posting your project and handling the backend that connects you with your backers, Kickstarter wants a percentage of your funds if you succeed . . . 5%. And Amazon, handling the e-commerce half of the deal, will take between 3% and 5% . . . and no, they don't explain what the criteria are for the difference, so it's best to assume 5%. So already you need to set your target 10% higher than your actual cost if you want to be able to afford your fabulous birding trip. And that's before your backer prize costs.

Your next task? To calculate the cost of those prizes. Everything you're offering to people in return for their support is going to cost you something: time or money (or both). At this point, make a list of all the fabulous prizes you've brainstormed or collected from other people's projects and write them down. For your birding extravaganza, your initial list might look like this:

1. Original painting of bird
2. Print of bird painting
3. Doodle of bird
4. Postcard from Alaska with thank-you note

Now it's time to calculate the costs for each of these rewards . . . to you, in time and money. I recommend a spreadsheet for this task (though you can build a grid on paper if you prefer), with a column for the prize, a column for how much it costs, and a column for how long it takes to create and send to someone. So, for our particular list, we come up with the following:

1. *Original painting of bird*
   - street value $50
   - Shipping: $35 with insurance in the US
   - Time to make: 4 hours—creation, documentation of the piece, packing for shipping, taking to mail place, et cetera
2. *Print of bird painting*
   - $10 to have printed, $10 to send to artist
   - Shipping: $10 to a backer in the US
   - Time: about an hour in random administrative tasks (ordering, packing, et cetera)
3. *Doodle of bird*
   - $20 street value
   - Shipping: $5 in the US
   - Time: about an hour to make/mail

4. *Postcard from Alaska with thank-you note*
   - $2 for postcard
   - Shipping: $0.50 in the US
   - Time: fifteen minutes to address and write out the note (after spending time looking up name, address, et cetera)

Your next step is to put a price on your time. Decide how much you need to be paid in order to be able to take time away from your job or other paying activities so you can make and send your Kickstarter prizes. For instance, if you're paid $9 an hour right now, then you should at least pay yourself that much. But let's go for $10 an hour, just for the round number.

Now look at your prizes and get the cost of your time for each prize:

1. original painting of bird: 4.00 hours $40
2. print of bird painting: 1.00 hour $10
3. doodle of bird: 1.00 hour $10
4. postcard from Alaska: 0.25 hour $2.50

Based on this, you can now decide where to place each of your prizes. Put them in order of cost and time spent and double the backer level on the cost—at least. You come up with the following:

1. original painting, cost of $125: prize for $250-level

backers
2. print of bird painting, cost of $40: prize for $80-level backers
3. doodle of bird, cost of $35: prize for $60-level backers
4. postcard from Alaska, cost of $5: prize for $10-level backers

This is not sticking it to people! You need to be able to cover the costs of the prizes you're offering people with enough to left over to actually pay for your project's goal. For that to work, every person who signs up has to be helping you pay for the project, and for that there has to be a "profit" on your cost to give them their goodies.

Now that you have some prizes, you can have a look at them as a whole. You want to give people with a lot of money something special; but you also want to give people with only a few bucks a reason to chip in. Kickstarter reports the most popular pledge level is $25, so you should have something around that level. But offering people a shout-out for less is fine as long as it doesn't cost you much. I see a lot of people offering a thank-you on a website in return for $5; I stuck a post-it note with people's names on the coffee they bought me with their $5 pledges and posted that photograph on the project blog. While I have yet to see a compelling prize that could be done for $1, people get pretty creative in the $5–10 level.

As much as possible, your lower-tier rewards should cost you the least in time and effort to provide . . . but you should have one or two if you can swing it. Try brainstorming some ideas. Virtual gifts are great for cheaper levels: physical products are costly to manufacture and ship. A digital photograph of a bird, or a scan of a bird people can use as a phone background or social media icon . . . that's cheap. Plus, you only have to make it once, and then you can pass it out to all your low-level backers. So throw in something like that for your bird project:

1. *$5 prize:* bird doodle, screen resolution, to be used as social media icon. (Cost: $5, for the half hour it took you to scan and crop it.)

So now you have the following levels:

$5: bird icon
$10: postcard
$40: print
$60: doodle
$250: original painting

At this point, you can spend some time finessing the results. You want a $25 level prize, for instance, to take advantage of what Kickstarter reports to be the most popular pledge level. You might also want to add in an extravagant pledge level . . . $500? $1000? What would you give someone who was willing to invest that much? And yes, why not put in a level that high? As my own backers have told me:

"I wouldn't think to do it unless you suggest it."

You can make some prizes more exciting and exclusive than others—and more cost-effective for you—by limiting the number you're offering, an option Kickstarter allows during set-up. For instance, if you'd like to excite people about your bird paintings, you might try offering 10 original paintings at a discount level of $150.

⇒ ◈ ⇐

A final consideration: while at this point only people in the US can use Kickstarter to *launch* projects, Kickstarter lets anyone in the world *back* projects . . . which means you may find yourself accidentally promising to mail something halfway across the world. It's typical to either ask international backers to add extra money to cover their mailing costs on physical prizes, or to set up separate backer levels for international backers who are claiming the same prize as American supporters but who have to pay extra to receive them.

Scheduling

Prizes aren't the only thing that needs planning . . . the length of your campaign and its start and end dates need to be planned as well. Yes, scheduling matters! There are many factors involved in scheduling of your campaign: length, dates and your personal calendar.

Length

Kickstarter lets you run a campaign for anywhere between one day and sixty. Some things to consider then:

Long campaigns allow you to hit multiple pay periods. People with standard jobs are usually paid twice a month, either bimonthly or on specific calendar dates, usually the fifteenth and last day (or first day) of the month. Kickstarter will charge people on the final day of the project if it's successfully concluded, so if you want to run your campaign for a month (or two, the full sixty), you can give people between one to four paychecks' worth of luxury money to set aside for you.

Long campaigns are ideal for projects for which you have planned a lot of media attention. If, for instance, you have contacts in radio, newspaper, podcasting, TV or in the local news—or if you don't and are planning to pursue opportunities and interviews in the hopes of drumming up attention for your project—then you want a longer campaign in order to give the media time to produce the segment and air it. Realistically, you should be lining those opportunities up in advance of your launch to allow for long lead-times, but a two-month campaign gives you more wiggle room if you find an opportunity during the project.

However, long campaigns take a lot of energy to run. If you don't think you can sustain your enthusiasm, day after day, for thirty to sixty days, it's better to keep the project duration short.

Dates

You also should plan carefully for when your campaign begins and ends. The high traffic days for most websites are Monday and Tuesday. You'll want to start your campaign on one of those days, and if possible, end it on one of those days also, so that you can get the largest number of people at their keyboards hitting "reload" in the final minutes of your campaign.

You should also choose the time carefully. Unless you have a significant international fanbase, plan for an American audience. If your project has heavy local interest, then you'll want to keep the time you launch and the time you end during the conventional work-day (and not during lunch). If your project is broader in scope, pick a time that works for you, but also allows backers throughout the US to keep an eye on your project without having to be up too late or too early.

In addition to the day and time, the date matters. Don't begin or end your project during major holidays or long weekends. If your creative field has big trade shows or conventions, don't schedule your project to begin or end during one of them when your fans will be away doing other things. For instance, if you're launching a graphic novel project, grab a calendar and find out where all the people into comic books are going to be in the next few months . . . and plan around that. (If you can schedule your project so that one of those major events happens during your campaign, allowing you to capitalize on backers and fans taking word of what you're doing to other potentially interested people . . . by all means! Do so!)

Your Schedule
So we've talked about everyone else's schedule, and how long you'll be running your campaign, and when. Now let's talk about your schedule . . . and yes, you're going to have one. Running your campaign—just running it, not actually doing the creative project it's supposed to be funding—will use up anywhere from 20 minutes to an hour a day, every day. And that's assuming you don't have any interviews/big media pushes scheduled! So don't plan on running a campaign while you're traveling, slammed with other work, having a baby, helping with family events, etc. Avoid holidays, too. You're going to be working on this thing every day for 10-60 days! Not only that, but the work's only part-done when your Kickstarter concludes . . . then you actually have to go out and do the thing you've promised, and send all the prizes out. The fulfillment phase following a successful Kickstarter can take anywhere from two weeks to half a year . . . or longer, if you're actually going to Alaska to paint birds. So be realistic, and plan accordingly!

Multiple Projects
. . . And since we're talking about energy level . . . I recommend not running more than one campaign at a time, unless you have an excess of it, and the projects have very different audiences. If you're looking for funding for a

fashion project and a gaming project, that's probably safe. But don't do two novels, or two art projects. Your backers are only going to have so much money, and if they have to choose between more than one cool-looking project by you they're not going to have enough to do both, or they'll split their pledges and you'll run the risk of neither funding.

Save your energy and keep that second project in the wings for when you're done with the first.

Writing the Story

So you've chosen your prizes, planned your schedule, and now you're up to the next big step of launching a successful Kickstarter: the Story. This is the part people see beneath your video where you explain what you're doing and why they should be excited about it. It pays to use this space to be personable, enthusiastic and direct about what you're trying to accomplish and why you think it's cool. As always, the best place to start is research. Go to the Kickstarter site and surf around. Look at projects with underwhelming Stories—what about them turned you off? Was it the grammar/spelling? Was the Story too short? Did it not give you examples? Did it ramble? Did you understand what the project creator was trying to accomplish? Did they give you the sense that they knew what they were talking about and were likely to deliver on their project?

Look now for projects with Stories that intrigued you. What about them spoke to you? Did they make you laugh?

What tone did they have? How long were they? How did the creators lay out their ideas? What kept you reading?

For me, what makes a good Story is variable. I find that if the project is something I'm already interested in (I like science fiction, for instance), the Story doesn't have to blow me out of the water as long as I can tell what the creators are doing and it looks interesting. But if I'm *not* into what the creator's trying to fund, the Story matters a great deal. I've backed projects I didn't actually want any prize from just because the Story was intriguing, compelling or just plain witty. I can appreciate someone who makes me laugh—that's worth a cup of coffee to me.

This is an interesting data point, as I'm not the only person I know who does this. It's completely possible to win people over, even if it's only to hand you a dollar or two, just by making an effort to be funny, enthusiastic or by looking super-competent.

I've also noticed some things that catch my eye: when creators use quotes from other people in their Stories (particularly from famous people, or big names within the project's field), that interests me. When Stories have extra photographs/images, that's engaging. Having an easy-to-read Story, with lots of breaks for headings, paragraphs and lists . . . that makes it more likely I'll keep reading.

I also notice that, for my part, I like a summary at the beginning: give people a quick overview on the project's purpose and why it's awesome. You hook them in the beginning, then explain the details.

Your list of what's compelling might be different from mine . . . or not! So do the research and look around, both in your category and other categories, until you've gotten a fairly big list of items that worked for you and didn't. Use those as guidelines to write a project Story that would interest you. Chances are, if it works for you, it will work for other people. But just in case . . . show it to a few friends first. Kickstarter will give you a preview link to your project before you launch it for just this purpose, so show it around and ask for impressions.

Video

Here is the point where I get to confess my own ignorance. I'm not a big video person. In fact, with rare exception, I never watch the videos associated with Kickstarter projects. I'm not even at a computer with speakers most of the time!

But I am overwhelmingly in the minority, and if, like me, you're not a big video person, you are in the minority also. And neither of us can afford to ignore the importance of a video to a Kickstarter project; according to Kickstarter, projects with videos are 50% more likely to succeed, compared to only 30% for those without. Twenty percent is a big difference when you're fighting for every dollar. So by all means . . . let's talk movies!

In my own experience, I have found videos have a big effect on my projects. While I am no good judge of how well my videos turn out, Kickstarter helpfully provides statistics about how many people clicked on your video and how many of them finished watching it. I found that projects where people were more likely to finish the video were also more likely to collect funding (!). So it's completely possible to turn people onto what you're up to just with your video alone, and convert that interest into backers.

So you need a video. And as someone not good with video, I am in no position to explain to you how to go about making one. From my observation, your choices are to do it professionally, polished and composed—either because you're a film person yourself or you know someone/are hiring someone for that purpose—or to do it as obviously personal and casual as possible. "One person behind a webcam" is surprisingly effective because it makes you more approachable, more believable as "just another person trying to do something awesome."

Since I am horrible with video, instead of giving advice I will share my stories with you; having done four Kickstarters (and planned a fifth, unlaunched, with finished video), I have had to do this five times despite not being good with film *and* being terribly camera-shy. I have a webcam to train on my hands while doing livestreams . . . not on my face! But Kickstarter said I needed videos, so there unto the breach went I. . . .

In my first, I decided to go for the "Just Another Person with Webcam" personal story. I wrote a script to read and discovered quickly that reading from a script while on camera makes you look stilted and worse, your eyes aren't actually on the web camera, and that means you look like you're looking off to one side . . .

. . . Needless to say, that didn't work well. But I really needed the script to keep from babbling, so I printed it out in a giant font, cut it until it was short enough to fit on one page, and propped it up right under the web camera so my eyes were pointing in approximately the right place. And I got through it, and I was terribly nervous, and it took me four takes but I did it. Since my project was for a military science fiction novel with an unusual heroine, I wrote the script about why I'd chosen the heroine and why that should interest people, and yes, I kept it short. I seem to recall less than two minutes being recommended.

For my second project, a contemporary fantasy novel about Armageddon, I chickened out—I didn't want to get in front of the webcam *again*. So I made paper puppets, wrote a synopsis of the plot—basically a back of the book blurb—and then acted it out with the paper puppets. This worked a little better, though several of the puppets were so tall they got cut off in the video. Whoops. But at least I didn't have to look at the camera again!

For my third project, an art project where I promised to doodle things for people based on colors they chose, I went to the art store and used my phone camera to take video of a huge display of markers with all their delicious colors. Then I went home and edited it together with some scanned images of the kind of doodles I was planning to offer, with little text commentary fading in and out of the image to explain what we were looking at. I used the video editor that came with my copy of Windows, which is serviceable enough . . . but having no audio track was kind of weird . . .

. . . Nevertheless, I did it again for the fourth video, which I decided to do as a silent cartoon. It's for a web comic, so it seemed appropriate, but I have no animation tools at all. So I drew the cartoons and scanned them, and then laboriously built "frames" in it where the dialogue balloons slowly appeared. Then I pasted it together in the Windows video editor, putting the frames in order. The result looks a little like . . . well, a web comic, but as a video. I'm hoping that will go over well.

For the fifth video, for a project launching a fantasy of manners novel, I decided (with resignation) to go again for the webcam approach. This time I decided not to do the script, since figuring out how to get the right combination of trading glances between script and camera was too much stress for camera-shy me. I did plan what I was going to say, I just didn't write it down. And since I wasn't entirely sure how to describe the project without rambling, I decided not to; instead, I decided to discuss my "credentials," starting with the handwritten novel I wrote in seventh grade, which I showed everyone and then explained how I wouldn't be inflicting it on them. Then I brought out all the other novels I'd published and showed them to the camera. This video made a lot of people laugh, but I made some mistakes: I didn't speak loudly/clearly enough, and I should have had the book stack arranged better, so I could pick up each without fumbling for them.

So yes. This video thing . . . I'm not great at it, and I'm still figuring it out. Hopefully hearing how someone who isn't good with video managed will give you some thoughts about how to tackle it yourself . . . ! And if you want to see my efforts for yourself (God help me), they're all still available on Kickstarter via my profile (search for *mcahogarth*). You can have a look and learn from my mistakes . . . !

Planning for Unexpected Success

So, we've got our target, our schedule, our Story and video. Don't launch yet! Let's be confident and optimistic and plan for unexpected success. Why? Because if you do hit your goal, you're going to need to entice people to keep paying, and if you don't have ideas ahead of time your enthusiasm might lead you to promise things you can't deliver. Plus, there are considerations involved with unexpected success that you need to consider in advance of it actually happening. . . .

Stretch Goals

Having come up with your initial funding target, you can now make a list of additional monetary milestones. If you asked for $500, for instance, $750 or $1000 might be good targets. Your goal is to offer something at these milestones that will inspire people to want to keep funding (or telling their friends). Stretch goal prizes can be anything you can imagine that has to do with your project: I've seen publishing projects that offered hardcover editions at stretch goals, or added limited edition chapbooks; food projects that offered extra food; art projects that offered to ship postcards to all backers . . . whatever it is, it should both be exciting and (more importantly) affordable. Be creative! For my military science fiction novel, I offered patches as a stretch goal prize, with the unit sign for the team from the novel. I've done bookmarks as stretch goal gifts and extra stories set in the same universes or "cut scenes" from the novels in question. Go browsing the site for projects that have exceeded their funding but are still running (under the Popular category, for instance) and see what stretch goal prizes people are offering.

    The stretch goal gift is only half the equation. The other half is the stretch goal itself. People like to know what you're going to use your windfall of cash for! So set goals for yourself. Is your project an art project? Why not use extra money to buy that wonderful box set of supplies you've been eyeing for years? Is your project in fashion? Why not plan to buy a cupboard for fabrics? Get people involved: take photos of what you're planning to do with that money. Show people the options. Discuss why you want it, how you decided you needed it and what you plan to do with it. Get them excited about your opportunities ... and the rewards you hope to offer if you reach a certain threshold over your target.

So, once again, haul out your spreadsheet. Put in a column for things you'd like to have if you get extra money. Then put in a column for things you could give people if you hit that goal. Once again, calculate how much it would cost you to get your goodie for yourself—if a new computer is going to cost you $800, then your stretch goal needs to be able to cover that cost, and extra for the Kickstarter/Amazon percentage and the amount you need to fulfill your prizes. Once again, calculate the cost of the prizes you are going to offer people. Then make a list of possible Exciting! New! Goals! that you can offer if you overfund. If you tell people you've mapped these out in advance, it's far more likely they'll be excited. Part of the fun of a Kickstarter is the anticipation, the not-knowing: will the project fund? By how much? Will there be more prizes? What will they be! What will the creator do next?? Let's watch! Let's get involved!

Administrative Overhead

So you are prepared with a list of stretch goals and stretch goal prizes. Your next task is to consider the administrative costs of unusual success. Say you're anticipating maybe twenty or thirty people to fund your Kickstarter. What will you do if fifty show up?

A hundred?

A *thousand*?

This is where the time-to-fulfill part of the equation (which you calculated during the design phase) is so important. Write up some scenarios where you're having to send prizes to unexpected numbers of people and see what it does to your schedule. Did you promise that you'd have all the prizes out within two weeks? Is that still do-able if you have fifty people to ship to, rather than twenty-five? How much longer will it take you?

Be prepared to move your delivery dates if you have an unexpected number of backers. You'll have to keep them informed, but if you do so with confidence (and excitement—after all, you're having to push the schedule back because so many people want your stuff!), you'll find people will be sympathetic.

⇒ ⦀ ⇐

. . . But what if you don't want to deal with that much overhead . . . or just can't?

How to Cap Your Funding

While it seems counterintuitive to want to aim for less money, there will be times when you really just want a specific amount and no more—usually when you don't have the time to manage the fulfillment of a large number of prizes. There are several ways you can attempt to limit your project's scope.

First, you can choose a short campaign run time: one week, ten days, fifteen . . . but less than a month, certainly. The shorter the duration, the less time people will have to spread news of the project around.

You can make sure all your prizes are easy (not much effort) for you to produce and send out; for instance, have them be all virtual items like digital artwork, e-books, anything that doesn't require physical manufacture and mailing.

You can make sure all your goals are quick (not very time-consuming) for you to produce and send out: for instance, instead of mailing out separate little original works, you can mass-produce postcards and mail those instead.

You can set small funding targets: $100, for instance, rather than $1000.

You can limit the number of awards available at each level, so, say only allowing ten people per backer level.

Having said all this, however, I will finish by noting there's never a guarantee. My most overfunded project ran for only ten days and asked for only $300 . . . and overfunded by almost 600%. I was anticipating doing doodles for ten to fifteen people . . . and fifty-three showed up.

I did a *lot* of drawing in the following month . . . !

Chapter Three Questions

1. Are there other projects out there similar to mine? What are they doing that I like? What don't I like?

2. How much money will I need to do my project? Is it a reasonable amount? How can I keep it small and likely-to-fund? Have I added in Kickstarter and Amazon's percentages to my costs?

3. What prizes can I offer? Have I seen other prizes out there that look interesting? Could I afford to offer similar ones?

4. Do I have a good spread of prizes ranging from the least expensive to the extravagant?

5. Have I double-checked to make sure I can afford to send out those prizes, even if I get more people than I expect backing? Did I make sure the lowest-level prizes were also the least costly to produce and send?

6. Did I remember to take into account international backers?

7. Did I choose a good length for my campaign based on how much I need to raise?

8. Did I schedule to begin at a good time and date, and to end on one?

9. Are there any major holidays or events that might mess up my schedule?

10. Is my schedule clear enough for me to throw myself into a ten- to sixty-day commitment?

11. Did I look around Kickstarter for examples of compelling Stories, and take notes on them?

12. Did I write a short, punchy summary for my project to go at the top?

13. Did I keep the Story interesting, as brief as I could, and as personable as I could? Did I check the spelling and grammar? Did I let some people have a look at it before launch?

14. Do I want to do the video myself or ask for help?

15. If I did it myself, did I look at the camera and speak clearly? Did I keep it short?

16. Did I make a list of stretch goals and prizes? Did I price them out for cost to me?

17. Have I thought about whether I can handle unexpected success? What will it take for me to get my prizes to twice the number of people I expect? Five times?

Running the Campaign

Before You Begin

YOUR PROJECT IS READY. You have the green launch button, and your cursor is hovering over it—

—Stop!

You have one task to do before you launch: go out and fund a few other projects.

Now, I know, I really do know, that the reason you're launching this project is because you *have no money*. You're on the site to convince other people to buy you a sandwich before you starve to death over your keyboard, mixing board, design table or easel. I really, really do know that it's hard to find the money. But it's important not to look like—or be—one of those people who uses something for their own purposes, and heck with everyone else.

When I back a project, I check the creator's profile. I want to know if I can trust them. I want to know who they are and what they're like and what they've done. And one of the first sets of statistics I look at is how many projects they've created . . . and how many they've backed. If someone's only created a single project and backed none, I am vaguely disappointed but I figure they're just new to Kickstarter and haven't had a chance to look around yet. If they've created several projects and backed few—or none—I start feeling vaguely preyed upon. I want to see evidence of someone who cares about the community of creators, who can get excited about other people's success, because those are the kinds of people I want to support.

And when I talk to people who back projects, I discover... I'm not the only one. People give a lot more leeway to creators who are backers, and some people have even confessed that if they only have money for one project, then they'll often go with one whose creator has backed other projects. It can break the tie in their head: they want the person who cares about other people.

When I see someone who's created one project but has backed several, I am impressed and far more likely to support that person than I am to support someone who hasn't. And, as I mentioned, I'm not the only one.

Set aside your pin money for as long as it takes to scrape up a few dollars to put in other people's pockets. You don't have to throw a ton of money at it. Just go and buy someone a cup of tea or coffee, if you can. Chances are, if you start looking, you'll find people you really want to help anyway.

And Now . . . Launch! (or, Your Daily Schedule)
So, the project's ready to go, and you've found some projects to back. You're ready . . . hit *go!*

Now comes the hard work . . . actually running the campaign. I chose the word "running" on purpose, because it's that much effort. It's a lot like doing a job-hunt:

putting together a resume and dropping it on a job-hunt site is useless. You have to go out and pound the pavement. The two major ways you have of doing that are updates to the project blog and social media.

Project Updates

The feedback I've received from backers is that they like to see activity on the Kickstarter project itself. Frequent updates intrigue people: what's this person up to, what are they talking about? What's going on! While a lack of them leaves people wondering whether the project coordinator's as excited about the project as they're telling people *they* should be. I've noticed a lot more money comes in on the projects I am super-updatey about. Not only that, but I am far more invested in the success of projects I back that also update frequently. The most important dynamic in a Kickstarter project is the circuit between creator and backers; project updates are a way to feed that loop and keep the real heart of a Kickstarter alive.

So how do you stay on top of updates? I found that sitting down and making a list of topics and ideas is helpful. For example, my fiction project "ideas for updates" list included the following topics:

- *Layout:* Talk about the professional doing the work, the things I like in layout, what I'm looking to do with the layout/the feel I'm going for.
- *Info on audiobooks:* Talk about the producer, the pro-

cess. Talk about previous audiobooks in the same series. Get clips for download, or schedule livestreams to play clips.

- *Meta-conversations:* Talk between the characters and the author, or the characters and the fans.
- *Little ink drawings:* Show off some of the interior art.
- *World-building examples:* Talk about the constructed language created for the setting and its effect on writing the text.

So, assuming I didn't have news that day (like "we're hosting a livestream today" or "this new Kickstarter goal has been reached, and the incentive is now ready!"), I would pick something from that list and write about it just to keep us all excited. Kickstarter allows you to append video, sound files and images to your posted updates; I suggest using that whenever appropriate, whether it's adding a photograph of your workspace or your stacks of creative products just ready to be mailed to videos of you dancing with excitement over something. Engage people's senses! People respond to a variety of things, so try as many as you can!

While it's not necessary to update every day, people do notice your posting schedule. I've had backers tell me later that they looked forward to the update emails in their boxes every morning, and missed them when they didn't arrive. One backer even told me she didn't give as much to one specific project I ran because I wasn't as on top of the updates, so it just . . . slipped their mind to talk about it to their friends and keep up with it.

For my own sanity—even workaholics need rest—I make it a policy not to update on weekends unless something extraordinary happens; in one case, I hit a major milestone over a weekend and posted about it immediately. But every week-day, I update my projects. And if you decide five days a week is too much, at very least pick a schedule and stick to it. Don't be afraid about the notion of "spamming" people; they can always tick the 'don't email project updates' box.

Social Media

Your other important daily task is the social media hit; it's handy to do this part after you make an update to the Kickstarter project, so you can link to the update. Choose one of your social media outlets to receive daily updates on your project, and then save the other outlets for occasional or "I'm excited!"-announcements. Blog, Twitter, Facebook, wherever your fans are, there you should go. If your big social media outlet is a podcast, then by all means, talk about it there! Or schedule Google hangouts or Skype chats . . . whatever works for you and the people interested in what you're doing. Current statistics show that Facebook drives a lot of traffic to Kickstarter projects, but if you don't have a Facebook account (or aren't active on it), don't despair . . . if you have family and fans who are, they'll probably use their Facebook accounts to mention you, when you ask.

At some point, you will be tempted to wonder if you're overdoing the social media advertisements. And it is easy to do that, particularly if you use the same format every time you talk about it: repeating "Come back my fashion project on Kickstarter!" every few hours will get you unfollowed, certainly. Vary your updates; use them to reflect your project's status. Try: "We're only thirty percent from goal! See what's got people excited about my fashion project on Kickstarter!" or "Today on my Kickstarter project blog: all about fabrics appropriate for lining corsets!" Etc. Give people something specific to investigate and talk about.

Likewise, give your fans something specific to do. They backed your project because they believed in what you were doing... or, at very least, because they were intrigued by it. They want to feel involved, like their contribution matters. And it does! Word-of-mouth funds Kickstarter projects, so don't be afraid to ask people to spread your project to their friends, ask them to pass along opportunities for interviews or news spots, tell them when you're almost at some awesome goal, and could they please help you find the last $100/5%/ten backers to meet whatever goal you're aiming for.

Your backers are your partners. Listen to what they've got to say and ask for their help.

Other Activities
If you're planning a big campaign or just want to experi-

ment, your other tasks can be everything from wandering around local universities or other places where creative people gather and hanging fliers to soliciting interviews and ads from news places. If you're feeling experimental, you could try issuing press releases or running web ads . . . anything you can think of to spread the word! Budget for it (time and money) and give it a try, see what works for you.

The other thing you can do while running your campaign is . . . do some of the actual project. If you're worried that it won't fund, you can hold back. But the moment you do fund, whether you have a day left or twenty, you should either be starting on the project or have it in progress, even if it's just the planning stages. The more you can have done before the campaign concludes, the faster fulfillment will go . . . and the faster you can move on to your next project!

Things That Affect Your Campaign as You Run It

I mentioned a while back that you can only expect 10% (maximum) new people to find your project through Kickstarter unless you win the publicity lottery. There are some factors that jiggle that percentage, some in your control and some not:

Everyone wants to be a Staff Pick! It gets you on top of the page for your category and singles you out as particularly promising to browsers. All that sounds great until you realize that every day all of the Kickstarter employees are looking for Staff Picks. You'll be at the top of the page for a few days and then fall off as they find new projects to highlight. You can't count on that to get you super-abundant attention. It's a nice boost, briefly, but it's not going to fund your project.

Activity, however, will get you noticed for as long as you inspire it. High-activity projects, those that get a lot of backers at a time, end up on "Popular This Week," which tends to stick longer. People check the "Popular This Week" because they're curious what other people are excited about. If you overfund or if one of your updates gets you a spate of new backers at a time, then you can end up on "Popular This Week" for quite a while.

The "Popular" statistic can also cause Kickstarter's algorithms to start suggesting you to people who fund projects similar to yours and that often results in click-throughs. It pays to hustle!

Related to activity level, success interests people. I got more strangers backing the more over-funded my project was. This makes sense; I notice that when browsing I tend to be more curious about projects either with lots of backers or extreme overfunding. This suggests that keeping your project as lean as possible can be a strategy for success. If the minimum you need to do what you want is $300 and there's another $700 of "would be nice"s, then set the target at $300 and plan prizes for overfunding to reach those other goals.

Finally, *remember*: If you are not super-excited about your project, your fans and random passersby won't be either.

Chapter Four Questions

1. Did I back some projects before I launched mine?

2. Did I make a list of updates I can write about when I don't have news?

3. Did I pick an update schedule?

4. Did I make a daily task list for myself so I can keep on top of the campaign and any creative work I want to do prior to the Kickstarter's completion?

5. Have I hit my social media today?

6. Am I keeping my updates topical, and giving people something to discuss beyond the existence of the project?

7. Am I hunting actively for other opportunities, like ads, interviews, guest blogs, etc?

Fulfillment

You have run your campaign, it's successfully funded and . . . now you have money! Lots of money!

And . . . a lot of responsibility.

Kickstarter does not police its project creators to make sure they make good on the promises they make to backers. If you don't send them the prizes they paid for, Kickstarter's not going to chase you down and make you. Which makes it all the more important that you do what you say you will. If you want any hope at all of continuing to use Kickstarter as a funding source in the future, you have to establish a reputation for being dependable.

So, start now! Keep your backers updated on your progress on their rewards. If there are set-backs, be honest about them; hiding them will only create uncertainty (and later, anger). Pick an update schedule a little less intense than the one you used during your campaign and send your backers regular updates until you're done sending all your prizes. Your updates don't have to be long . . . even a photograph of your living room floor covered in boxes and envelopes can say enough! But stay on top of things and keep going until it's done.

While you're working, track your actual expenses—you can use the same spreadsheet you made to track your projected expenses—so you have an idea of how close to your targets you were. If buying envelopes cost you more than you anticipated, you'll need that information in the future if you ever do something similar. You often pay dearly for experience, so write it down so you won't have to pay it again!

And one final important task: track your income. Kickstarter money is not charity money... you will be required to report it for tax purposes. So keep careful accounting of how much you collected, how much you spent and how much you took away at the end of the project. You'll need to plug those numbers into your books when you do your reporting come April fifteenth.

But What If I Failed?

Did your Kickstarter not fund? Don't give up! Like most things, running a campaign requires practice. People who get it right the first time are usually people with business and marketing experience who have a good sense for how to capitalize on opportunities to raise capital. If you don't have that experience, the only way to get it is by trying again.

Have a look at your project and do some troubleshooting. Did you not get enough backers? You may not have made your Story compelling enough, or your prize levels didn't encourage people to give you money. Did you get backers but not enough money? Maybe your prizes at the higher levels weren't enticing enough. Did you get backers and money, but not hit your goal? You might have set your funding goals too high... try for something smaller.

Or maybe your campaign did fund . . . but it cost you more money to make good on your promises than you made. Track your expenses and see where the problems started cropping up. The more you know about the cost of doing business, the better your projections will be in the future.

Finally, your best resource is to ask your backers what they think about why the project didn't work for them. Listen to them without judging: they are an important resource. They might tell you anything—that your video turned them off, that they would have backed at a higher level but didn't like the prizes, that your updates didn't inspire them—but whatever it is, the feedback is valuable. When they're done giving you their impressions, thank them and go do more research on the site. If your video failed for your viewers, check out some Popular projects and see how they did theirs. If they found the prizes uninspiring, then go research prizes on similar projects again. But most of all, listen to what they've got to say. If they donated even a dollar to your project, they cared enough about it to want it to succeed. Their critiques are coming from their desire to help you.

I remember one backer critique that made a huge difference to my first Kickstarter project and all the ones after it: I had launched a project to fund the print edition of a science fiction novel, and he commented (kindly but with a bit of a nudge) that I had not offered the print book as a prize. "Perhaps you might want to give backers a chance at the thing you're funding," he said. "Not all of us read e-books." So I put in a prize level for an autographed copy of the print book and that day my funding doubled. The print book prize in my fiction projects continues to be among my most popular, even when I'm offering other editions. To this day I remain deeply grateful to that backer for hitting me (gently) over the head over a mistake that should have been obvious . . . but wasn't.

Chapter Five Questions

1. Have I thanked my backers for their support?

2. Have I picked a new update schedule so I can keep my backers apprised of developments in the project?

3. Have I tracked all the actual expenses so I can compare them to my projected ones?

4. Have I tracked my income so I can report it at tax time?

5. Did I send out all my prizes in a timely manner? If I didn't, did I inform my backers of the setbacks immediately? Did I make a note of what held me up so I could plan for it in the future?

All Done? Do It Again

So you've concluded your first campaign, taking it from a spark in your brain all the way to packages in the mail and (hopefully!) the occasional pleased email or message from recipients who remembered to tell you that it was awesome.

Why not do it again?

Yes, I know, you're exhausted right now. But give yourself a month to rest, and I bet in less than that you'll already be wondering whether your latest idea could be transformed into a compelling Kickstarter project. The process becomes addictive: it's *exciting* to connect with your fans and with complete strangers and find out that, yes! They want to help you succeed! They really do want to be your partners in your career.

So yes! Capitalize on your success. Keep your name out there. Practice. Try new things. Write notes about what worked . . . and what failed. Keep researching; see what other people are doing. Check out the most successful projects. Let them inspire you. And continue generating your projects, and backing other projects, and being involved.

There's a world out there for your ideas, waiting to be won by you, one person at a time. Take a deep breath . . . and keep going.

Checklist from Spark to Finish

Idea Phase
1. Think of an *urge*
2. Think of *creative products* based on that urge
3. Think of the *story* about why this will be exciting
4. Find a Kickstarter *category* that fits.

Me Phase
1. Am I excited about this? Like, jump-up-and-down excited?
2. Am I willing to put in ten to sixty days of daily work on it?
3. Are my project goals realistic based on my fanbase?
4. How can I make my goals smaller/more nimble/easier to fund?

Design Phase
1. *Research:* What other similar projects are funding now?
2. *Calculate costs*
    a. How much to actually do what I'm planning?
    b. Kickstarter/Amazon fees: 10%
3. Come up with *prizes*
4. Calculate *costs* on *prizes*
5. *Set prize levels*
6. Decide on *additional prizes* to round out your offerings

7. *Schedule* your project
    a. Did you choose a good weekday to launch/end?
    b. Did you choose a good time?
    c. Is it good for your schedule?
    d. Are there any major events/holidays in the way?
8. Write the *story*
    a. Research other project stories.
    b. Start with an overview.
    c. Keep it easy-to-read, excited and personable.
    d. Add quotes, images and headers if you can.
9. Make a *video*
    a. Hire someone or—
    b. Keep it intimate and friendly.
    c. Make sure you speak clearly and look at the camera.
    d. Keep it under two minutes.
10. Design *stretch goals and prizes*
11. Calculate *costs* on stretch goals and prizes

After Launch
1. *Back* other projects before you begin, between one and five
2. Make *list* of update topics
3. *Update* on a regular schedule, and when something exciting happens
4. Offer *stretch goals and prizes* when you meet your target
5. Update *social media* daily
6. Look for other *media opportunities*

Fulfillment Phase
1. Get to *work* on your project!
2. Choose *new update schedule*
3. *Keep* your backers in the loop.
4. Make a commitment to *quality* and *transparency*
5. Get those *prizes out*
6. *Track* your expenses and compare them to your projections.
7. *Track* your income for tax purposes.

Final Phase
1. *Rest*!
2. Consider *new ideas*
3. *Research*
4. Do it again!

Would you prefer your questions worksheets and checklist as PDF downloads? I've got them on my website! Head to mcahogarth.org and choose the Three Jaguars tab. You'll find the downloads there, along with my other columns on doing business as a creative professional. No charge . . . just use them For Good!

About the Author

IT'S TRADITIONAL TO WRITE these sections in third person, but it does sound funny. So I won't! I—M.C.A. Hogarth—am an author of over fifty titles in the genres of science fiction, fantasy, humor and romance, as well as a fantasy painter . . . but I've had my foot in the business world all my life, and translating between the business and creative worlds has been one of my most exciting projects. For years I've been writing an occasional business column for creative professionals, The Three Jaguars. I also give seminars on new payment models for artists, having used crowdfunding to put food on my table since 2004, before it was even a word! And I offer business consultation for artists of every stripe.

If you've enjoyed this guide, I encourage you to check out my website. The Three Jaguars tab will link you to all my business columns—which are illustrated with cartoon jaguars, thus the name—and give you news and updates about the forthcoming web comics. If you'd like to look me up on Kickstarter, you'll find me under user mcahogarth. You can check out my previous projects, see if any of the methods, prizes or processes work for you. And yes, if they work for you, run with them!

And as always, I'd love to hear from you! Write a comment or a tweet or drop me a line. Tell me about your projects. We're all in this together: let's fill the world with amazing art.

mcahogarth.org
mcahogarth@twitter.com
haikujaguar@livejournal.com

www.ingramcontent.com/pod-product-compliance
Lightning Source LLC
Chambersburg PA
CBHW061518180526
45171CB00001B/238